Mail Merge for Beginners
MAIL MERGE ESSENTIALS BOOK 1

M.L. HUMPHREY

SELECT TITLES BY M.L. HUMPHREY

WORD ESSENTIALS
Word for Beginners
Intermediate Word

MAIL MERGE ESSENTIALS
Mail Merge for Beginners

EXCEL ESSENTIALS
Excel for Beginners
Intermediate Excel
50 Useful Excel Functions
50 More Excel Functions

CONTENTS

Introduction 1

Step 1: Create Your Source File 3

Step 2: Create Your Letter Template 5

Step 3: Start Your Mail Merge 7

Step 4: Link to Your Source File 9

Step 5: Insert Customized Fields Into the Template 11

Step 6: Preview Your Mail Merge 17

Step 7: Fixing Errors or Issues 19

Step 8: Finalize the Mail Merge 21

Other Thoughts and Comments 23

Conclusion 25

Appendix A: Basic Terminology 27

INTRODUCTION

This guide is for anyone who wants to learn how to perform a basic mail merge in Microsoft Office. The focus will be on how to merge an Excel-based mailing list into a Word-based template, so you should have a basic familiarity with both Word and Excel before using this guide.

We'll cover how to use a mail merge to create customized letters, envelopes, and mailing labels.

For those of you not familiar with what a mail merge is, it essentially takes a list of information and combines that with a template to create customized letters. If you've ever received one of those notices from your doctor's office reminding you of your annual check-up, you've probably received a letter created via a mail merge.

While you can also create customized email messages or use an Outlook contact list to create a mail merge, we will not address that in this guide. This guide is going to focus on a beginner-level mail merge using Excel and Word. (Mostly because I don't have a beginner's guide to Outlook that I could send you to if you're not familiar enough with Outlook. But once you've mastered the basics of a mail merge, doing so with Outlook shouldn't be all that much more difficult than doing so with Excel. If you're not familiar with Word or Excel, check out Word for Beginners or Excel for Beginners. Those should cover the basics you need to know to do a mail merge.)

These instructions are written based on Excel and Word 2013. If you're working in a version of Microsoft Office prior to the 2010 version, portions of this guide likely will not work for you although Word has had a mail merge option since at least the early 1990's. (Because I have vague memories of using it back then.) The principles of how it works have remained the same, but where you go and how you do things has changed.

Alright, then.

Let's get started.

STEP 1: CREATE YOUR SOURCE FILE

You may already have a source file that you can use, in which case you can skip this step. But if you don't, then you'll need all of the information you want to use in your mail merge available in an Excel spreadsheet.

Now, I will note here that Word can actually work with a variety of file types. In their help text Microsoft states that, "Word easily accepts data from Outlook, Excel, and Access, and other data sources such as web pages, OpenDocument text files, and delimited data files stored as plain text. And if you don't have an existing data source, you can create a new one in Word."

But for the basic type of mail merge we're going to discuss in this guide, we're just going to focus on using an Excel spreadsheet.

So if you don't have a source file yet, open Excel and create one. Be sure that all the data that you want to use in your mail merge is included and that your data is formatted properly.

Specifically, make sure that all of the information is in one worksheet (Sheet 1, for example) and that it is "clean". By clean, what I mean is that you should have a header row in the first row of your file that clearly labels the contents of each column and then one row per entry immediately below that with all of that entry's data in that one row.

There should be nothing else in your worksheet that you're using as your source file. So no subtotals, no extra spaces, no summary lines, and no comments or notes.

I'd also recommend that the descriptors you use in the header row be easy to understand. Don't have fields labeled "DVZN1" or something like that unless you know exactly what that means and so would other users, because when you insert the merge fields into your Word template those labels are all you'll see in the template.

Also, when using Excel make sure that any zip code entry is formatted as text instead of numeric, because Microsoft will drop zeroes from the front if you don't. For example, a zip code of 01234 will become 1234 if the field is formatted as numeric.

When you're done you want something that looks like this:

	A	B	C	D	E	F	G	H	I
1	Salutation	First Name	Last Name	Street Address	City	State	Zip	Next Visit Due	
2	Mr.	Bob	Jones	123 Perfect Drive	Anywhere	ID	12345	5/15/2019	
3	Ms.	Nancy	Clark	452 Snowy Way	Peace	PA	23456	6/15/2019	
4	Miss	Mattie	Marks	678 Jefferson Pkwy	Creek	CA	01234	7/15/2020	
5	Miss	Mattie	Marks	678 Jefferson Pkwy	Creek	CA	01234	8/1/2019	
6									

See how for each customer I have all of their information on one line? And how the header row makes it clear what the content is in each column? And how there are no extra lines between my header row and my data? And no subtotals or comments or extraneous information in the worksheet other than my customer data? That's what you want.

Once you have your file ready, save it somewhere permanent. In other words, save it to a location where you plan to keep it because once you link your Word template to the Excel file you won't want to move or rename the Excel file. That will break the link between the two documents and you'll have to relink them before you can complete your mail merge. (It's not the end of the world if that happens, it's just annoying and you may not realize that's what's causing you a problem.)

STEP 2: CREATE YOUR LETTER TEMPLATE

The first type of mail merge we're going to walk through is a letter mail merge. This is that form letter that the doctor's office sends customers reminding them it's time for their next visit.

(You can also create labels or envelopes using a mail merge, but we'll get to those later.)

If you're doing a letter mail merge, the next step is to create your form letter. What do you want to say to all of your customers? And what customized information do you want to insert into that letter and where do you want to insert it?

There are two ways to do this. One is to write the letter first and just use placeholders where you'll want a customized field. The other is to link your data file immediately and insert merge fields as you write the document.

I'm weird, so I tend to write the letter first using < > brackets around where I want customized text and then I go through and replace the bracketed text with the merge fields later. Probably a carryover from the days when I needed someone to approve a letter before I completed the mail merge.

If you do it my way, just open Word and write your letter. It'll end up looking something like this:

<Date>

<Salutation> <First Name> <Last Name>
<Street Address>
<City>, <State> <Zip Code>

Dear <Salutation> <Last Name>:

We are writing to inform you that you are due for your annual check-up on <Next Visit Date>. Please call our office at 123-456-7890 to schedule an appointment at your earliest convenience.

Sincerely,

Your Doctors

If instead you want to insert the mail merge fields as you write the document, then skip to the next step. Also use the next step for label or envelope mail merges. No need to write a template for those.

STEP 3: START YOUR MAIL MERGE

To tell Word that the document you're working on is going to be part of a mail merge, go to the Mailings tab, and choose an option from the Start Mail Merge dropdown in the Start Mail Merge section.

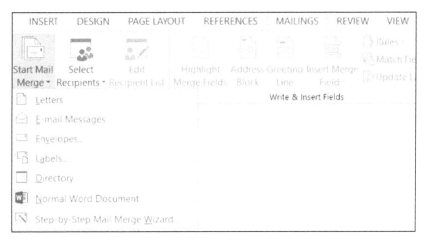

The options in the dropdown are pretty straight-forward. Letters will let you create a standard letter or Word document. The E-Mail Messages option will let you create an email message. The Envelopes option allows you to create the address portion of an envelope. Finally, the Labels option allows you to create mailing labels.

Note that I'm not covering the email option in this guide, but here are how the other three work:

Letters

To create a mail merge that will generate a form letter (like the letter from the doctor's office I showed you above), select the Letters option from the dropdown menu.

When you do this, nothing will actually change on your screen. That's okay.

Envelopes

To create a mail merge where you're going to print customer addresses directly onto envelopes, choose the Envelopes option from the dropdown.

When you do this, Word will ask you what kind of envelope you're using and where you want the To and From addresses to be positioned on that envelope. As you adjust the position settings, the preview image will show what your envelope will look like. There's also a tab for telling Word how you're going to feed envelopes into your printer so that the information prints correctly onto the envelope.

After you make your selections and choose OK the document visible on your screen is going to change so that it looks like the front of an envelope instead of a sheet of paper. (It'll basically be shorter than a standard page for most envelope types.)

Labels

To create a mail merge where you're going to generate customized address labels, choose the Labels option from the dropdown. (This is probably also the option to use for name tags or table placards.)

When you do this, Word will ask what kind of labels you're trying to create. There is a dropdown menu where you can choose the name of the company who created the labels you're using and then a product listing below that where you can choose the exact product you're using so that the dimension of the labels you create are identical to the ones you're going to print on.

After you make your selection and choose OK, your Word document will look like nothing has changed, but note where the cursor is and that there's a small box with arrows pointing in four directions. Even though you can't see it, that little box indicates that there is a "table" in the document at this point in time and each cell in that table will have the same dimensions as your address label.

STEP 4: LINK TO YOUR SOURCE FILE

The next step is to link the Word document to your Excel source file. (Note here again, that if your source file is not an Excel file this should work much the same way, but I'm just covering linking to an Excel file in this guide.)

To link to your source file, click on the Select Recipients dropdown menu from the Start Mail Merge Section of the Mailings tab, and choose the Use an Existing List option.

On my computer Word goes to My Data Sources by default. This may or may not happen to you. Chances are you do not have your source file saved to that location, so just navigate to where you do have it saved, choose the file, and select Open.

This may or may not bring up a Select Table dialogue box. If it does, choose the worksheet where you have your data saved and be sure that the checkbox that says "First row of data contains column headers" is checked. (If you didn't use the first row for column headers, then uncheck this box.)

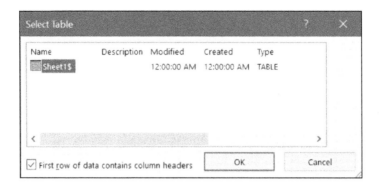

Click OK.

For the envelope and letter options, nothing will change in your document. For the labels option, you will see <<Next Record>> appear multiple times on the document. Don't worry about that, it's fine.

You should now be back in your Word document, but with your Excel data linked. The way to tell that you've successfully linked your data file to your Word document is to look at the choices under the Mailings tab. Edit Recipient List in the Start Mail Merge section as well as the choices in the Write & Insert Fields, Preview Results, and Finish sections should now be available to choose and no longer grayed out.

STEP 5: INSERT CUSTOMIZED FIELDS
INTO THE TEMPLATE

Now that you've linked your data source it's time to insert your merge fields into your document. These are the fields that will be customized for each customer/entry.

There are three options for doing this. You can use an Address Block, a Greeting Line, or you can insert any merge field anywhere in your document using the Insert Merge Field option. All three are available in the Write & Insert Fields section of the Mailings tab.

Let's start with the Address Block.

Address Block

The Address Block option is what you'll want to use for envelopes and address labels as well as for the address section of any letter you want to send.

What it does is provides the customer name and mailing address in the format that you choose.

To insert an Address Block into your document, click on the location in your document where you want to place the address block and then choose that option under the Write & Insert Fields section of the Mailings tab.

(For an envelope, be sure to click into the portion of the document where you'd expect the recipient's address to display. It by default will have your cursor located where your address should display.)

This will bring up the Insert Address Block dialogue box.

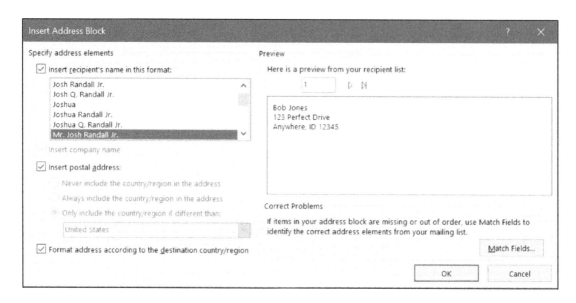

You can choose from a number of options for how to display the customer's name in the top left corner under where it says "Insert recipient's name in this format". Scroll down for options that include Mr. or Ms. in the name line.

For each option you select on the left-hand side, Word will display how that information will appear in your document using your source data on the right-hand side.

If Word doesn't recognize the label you've given a field, it will not display it. So, for example, in my sample data I used Salutation as the label for the field that contains Mr., Ms., Miss, etc. Word does not recognize that as a valid way to identify that field so when I choose an option that includes the Salutation, Word just leaves it out. I can see this in the preview. On the left-hand side it shows "Mr. Josh Randall, Jr." but in the sample on the right-hand side it shows "Bob Jones".

To tell Word which field to use for each data point, click on Match Fields in the bottom right corner of the dialogue box. This will bring up the Match Fields dialogue box where you can tell Word which field in your data source corresponds to the field names that Word uses.

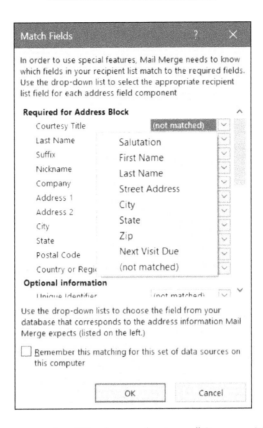

Here, for example, we can see that Word uses the term "Courtesy Title" for what I refer to as "Salutation". I simply click on the dropdown list next to Courtesy Title and select Salutation and now Word knows which field to use.

At the bottom of that dialogue box you can also see that there's an option to "Remember this matching for this set of data sources on this computer." If you're going to use that source file more than once, it can save you time to check that box because you'll only have to do this matching once.

Once your settings are to your liking, choose OK and Word will insert your Address Block into your document. At this point, you cannot see how that address has been formatted. It will just appear as <<AddressBlock>> in your document.

(Later we'll discuss how to use the preview option to see customer address information in your actual document.)

If you need to edit an Address Block after you've inserted it, right click on <<AddressBlock>> in your Word document and choose Edit Address Block from the dropdown menu. This will bring up the Modify Address Block dialogue box which looks exactly like the Insert Address Block dialogue box.

For envelopes and address labels, the Address Block is all you need, but for letters or for labels that are being used as name tags or some other purpose, there are two additional options. The next one is the Greeting Line.

Greeting Line

The Greeting Line option allows you to insert an introductory line such as "Dear Mr. Smith" at the beginning of a letter. It's better to use than creating your own introductory line using "Dear <Salutation> <Last Name>" because it will account for empty fields as well as use a generic introduction such as "To Whom It May Concern" if customer information is missing.

To insert a greeting line into your document, click on the location where you want it and then choose Greeting Line from the Write & Insert Fields section of the Mailings tab. This will open the Insert Greeting Line dialogue box.

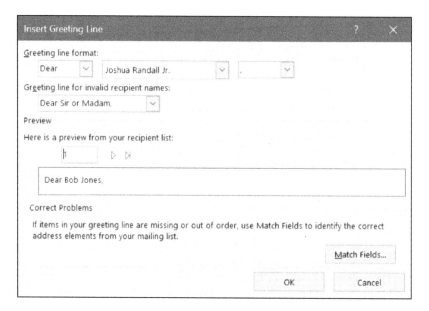

There are four choices to make with respect to the Greeting Line.

First, you can choose the introductory text to use. Your options are "Dear", "To", or to have no text used at all.

Second, you can choose how to display the contact's name information. There are a wide variety of formats such as John, Mr. Randall, Mr. John Randall, etc.

Third, you can choose whether to end the greeting line with a comma, a colon, or no punctuation at all.

So you could have a greeting line that looks like any of the following:

Dear John,

To Mr. and Mrs. Randall:

John

Your fourth choice is how to handle a situation where there is no customer name information available. Your choices are

Dear Sir or Madam,

or

To Whom It May Concern:

When using a Greeting Line be sure not to duplicate the punctuation. In the document itself you'll only see <<GreetingLine>> and not the punctuation that is part of that greeting line.

Insert Merge Field

Your final option is to insert a customized merge field. In our example letter from the doctor's office, we want one for the date of the customer's next visit.

In order to do this, the information you want to insert needs to already be in a column in the Excel data file you're using.

Click in the location in your document where you want to insert your merge field, go to the Insert Merge Field dropdown menu in the Write & Insert Fields section of the Mailings tab, and choose the field you want from the dropdown menu.

Today's Date

You may have noted that I didn't address yet how to insert today's date into your mail merge even though my sample letter had a date field at the top. If this is a letter template that you're using only once, then I'd just type in today's date. If it's a template that you want to use more than once and you want to make sure it always has the current date, then click on where you want the date displayed in your document, go to the Insert tab, choose Date & Time from the Text section, choose the date type you want to insert, making sure that the Update Automatically button is checked, and click OK.

(By clicking the Update Automatically button, every single time you open the document Word will update the date in the document to the current day's date. Whenever you use this field on a file be sure that's what you want to do and that the final version of the file that you save when it's actually sent is saved with the date finalized and no longer dynamic. I can't count the number of memos where I've seen this date feature used improperly and the original date of the memo was lost as a result.)

* * *

Once you're done with inserting all of your merge fields, scan the document to make sure that any placeholder text and any extra punctuation has been removed. You should end up with something that looks like this:

<Date>

«AddressBlock»

«GreetingLine»

We are writing to inform you that you are due for your annual check-up on <Next Visit Date>. Please call our office at 123-456-7890 to schedule an appointment at your earliest convenience.

Sincerely,

Your Doctors

Note how each merge field is marked with double arrows on each side.

STEP 6: PREVIEW YOUR MAIL MERGE

Before you generate your finalized merge file or print it, it's a good idea to preview the results. You can do this using the Preview Results section of the Mailings tab. First, click on Preview Results.

This will change the template document to show the first entry from your data source.

Scan the entry to see if it looks the way you want it to. Are there any weird spaces? Is there any strange or extra punctuation? Are there any missing spaces? What about the line spacing for the address block?

Basically, is the document as you see it on the screen what you wanted your document to look like?

If not, you'll need to turn off the preview by clicking once more on Preview Results and you'll need to go fix whatever issue you identified.

You can see what the document for each of your entries will look like by using the arrows in the Preview Results section. Click on the right arrow to move forward and the left arrow to move backward. Or, if you have a specific record in mind, you can enter the number of the record you want to review. Clicking on the arrows with a bar on the side will take you all the way to the beginning (for the left arrow) or all the way to the end (for the right arrow).

It's a good practice to thumb through your entire list of entries. But if you can't do that because there are too many then at least be sure to spot check examples where there is extra or missing information. So, for example, I'd want to check at least one that had a suffix on the name and one where the first name was missing.

STEP 7: FIXING ERRORS OR ISSUES

I don't like the default line spacing that Word uses for the address block and in my mailing labels example, I couldn't even see the full address on the label. Both of those are examples of where I would need to go back and fix the formatting before I could generate my final document.

To do this, go back to the version of your template that has the merge fields showing. (By clicking once more on Preview Results in the Preview Results section of the Mailings tab if you need to.)

To change paragraph or font spacing for an Address Block, right-click on the merge field name (<<AddressBlock>>), and choose Paragraph (for the paragraph spacing) or Font (for the font size). This will bring up the Paragraph dialogue box or the Font dialogue box, depending on which option you chose.

The spacing I prefer for the address line has values of 0 pt for before and after spacing and Single line spacing. (This also fixed the issue of the full address not appearing on my mailing label. If it hadn't I would have needed to change my font size to something smaller.)

* * *

Another issue you may run into is that the mail merge includes individuals you don't want to include. If that's the case, you can use the Edit Recipient List option under the Start Mail Merge section of the Mailings tab to amend the list of recipients. When you click on that option you'll see the Mail Merge Recipients dialogue box:

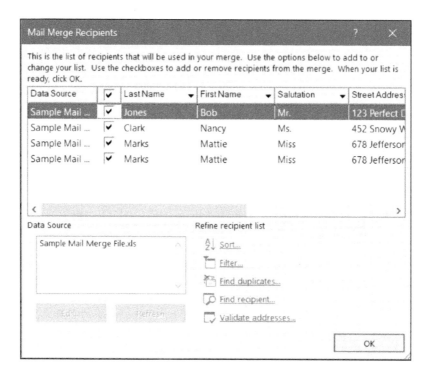

To exclude a single individual, just uncheck the box next to their name. There's also a Search function that makes it easy to find an individual if you already know the name.

You can also have Word identify duplicate entries for you by clicking on the Find Duplicates option in the bottom right section. When Word does that it will give you a list of apparent duplicates and you can then uncheck any records you don't want included in your merge.

You can also sort the list while in this dialogue box.

Or, if you have a large number of records that you want to exclude, you can use the filter option to do so. If you've filtered the list and later need to amend that, click on Filter again, and then choose Clear All to remove the filter or amend your filter criteria.

STEP 8: FINALIZE THE MAIL MERGE

Once you have everything looking the way you want it to, you need to actually finalize the mail merge. In this step, Word will generate a separate entry for each individual in your merge.

If you're working with labels, before you do this step click on Update Labels in the Write & Insert Labels section. Otherwise you're only going to generate your first address label and not any others. When you do this Word will carry over whatever merge fields you used in that first space to the rest of the spaces. In my example, it now reads <<Next Record>><<AddressBlock>> in each mailing label space.

To generate your final merged document, go to the Finish section of the Mailings tab and click on Finish & Merge. This will bring up a dropdown menu that allows you to either edit the individual documents, print them, or send them as email messages.

My preference when generating letters from a mail merge is to choose to Edit Individual Documents. What this does is creates a Word file that contains all of the letters I'm generating. It gives me one last chance to review the letters before I start wasting paper.

You can also choose the Print Documents option which will send your merged letters (or envelopes or labels) straight to your printer without generating an interim document.

Whichever option you choose, you will see either a Merge to New Document or Merge to Printer dialogue box. They look identical. It's one last chance to choose not to merge all of your records, but instead just merge a subset of them. Normally you would choose All at this step and then OK.

If you chose to Edit Individual Documents you will now see a Word document that contains all of your merged information. Each letter or envelope will start on a new page.

If you chose to Print Documents you will now see the Print dialogue box where you can choose which printer to use and how many copies to print.

If you do generate a Word document with all of your merged information, I recommend that you save that document when you're done so that you have a copy of the final letters that were sent.

(I'll note here that if you're generating letters that require a signature, you don't actually have to print those letters and have someone manually sign each one. You can have them sign a piece of paper for you, scan their signature, save that scan as an image, and then insert that scanned image of their signature into your template. That way when you do print the document it's already signed and you don't have to make some poor soul sign a hundred and fifty letters by hand.)

The final option in that list is for if you're sending a merged email, something we're not covering in this guide. That option is probably the most dangerous, because it's the easiest option for sending out a mistake before you can catch it.

OTHER THOUGHTS AND COMMENTS

When you create a Word mail merge template and link an Excel file to it, the next time you open the file you will get a scary looking message that looks something like this:

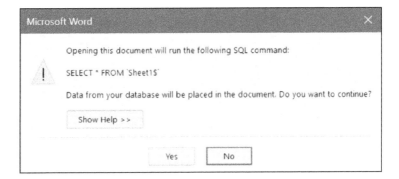

Go ahead and say Yes. That's just Office wanting your approval to keep the connection to the file that contains your data.

I will admit that the first time I saw that message I said No because it looked like something scary was going to happen if I said yes. If you do that, your document will still show the merge fields that you inserted, but all of the mail merge options in the Mailings tab will be grayed out and you won't be able to perform a mail merge until you reattach your data file.

To do so, just go to Select Recipients, Use an Existing List, and choose your data file once more.

You may also need to do this if at any point you rename or relocate the data file.

The nice news in either case is that you don't have to redo all of your data fields if that happens, you just need to link the two files once more. (If you ever change the name of a data field in your Excel file, that would very likely require having to reinsert that merge field into your document.)

* * *

Another issue I ran into while I was writing this up was when I wanted to amend my data file while I had the Word file open. I was not able to open and edit the Excel file. It was locked into a Read-Only mode while I had the Word file open.

There is an option to edit through Word, but I didn't trust using it and didn't see how it would easily let me add a new record. (I was trying to create a duplicate record at the time.)

If you run into this situation, I would recommend that you just close Word, open the Excel file, make the edits you need to make, and then reopen the Word file. That's the cleanest option in my opinion.

* * *

Another tip: If you're working with labels, you want to be sure that you get the right type at the beginning because if you later change the label type Word will erase any merge fields you've inserted into your document and start you over from scratch.

CONCLUSION

Alright, so there you have it. That's how to use Word and Excel to do a basic mail merge to create customized letters, envelopes, or mailing labels. As I mentioned at the beginning, you can also do mail merges using Access databases or Outlook contact lists and can do personalizing email mailings as well. While those were beyond the scope of this guide, they should work on the same principles.

If you get stuck, reach out. I'm happy to help if I can or track down an answer for you if I don't know it. You can reach me at mlhumphreywriter@gmail.com.

Also, Microsoft provides a number of great help resources on their website. They even have some videos that will walk you through mail merges. Just go to https://support.office.com and search for "mail merge using an Excel spreadsheet" to get started.

Best of luck with it!

APPENDIX A: BASIC TERMINOLOGY

TAB

I refer to the menu choices at the top of the screen (File, Home, Insert, Design, Page Layout, References, Mailings, Review, View, Developer) as tabs. If you click on one you'll see that the way it's highlighted sort of looks like an old-time filing system.

Each tab you select will show you different options. For example, if you have the Home tab selected you can do various tasks such as cut/copy/paste, format paint, change the font, change the formatting of a paragraph, apply a style to your text, find/replace words in your document, or select the text in your document. Other tabs give other options.

CLICK

If I tell you to click on something, that means to use your mouse (or trackpad) to move the arrow on the screen over to a specific location and left-click or right-click on the option. (See the next definition for the difference between left-click and right-click).

If you left-click, this selects the item. If you right-click, this generally creates a dropdown list of options to choose from. If I don't tell you which to do, left- or right-click, then left-click.

LEFT-CLICK/RIGHT-CLICK

If you look at your mouse or your trackpad, you generally have two flat buttons to press. One is on the left side, one is on the right. If I say left-click that means to press down on the button on the left. If I say right-click that means press down on the button on the right.

Now, as I sadly learned when I had to upgrade computers and ended up with an HP Envy, not all track pads have the left- and right-hand buttons. In that case, you'll basically want to press on either the bottom left-hand side of the track pad or the bottom right-hand side of the trackpad. Since you're working blind it may take a little trial and error to get the option you want working. (Or is that just me?)

SELECT OR HIGHLIGHT

If I tell you to select text, that means to left-click at the end of the text you want to select, hold that left-click, and move your cursor to the other end of the text you want to select.

Another option is to use the Shift key. Go to one end of the text you want to select. Hold down the shift key and use the arrow keys to move to the other end of the text you want to select. If you arrow up or down, that will select an entire row at a time.

With both methods, which side of the text you start on doesn't matter. You can start at the end and go to the beginning or start at the beginning and go to the end. Just start at one end or the other of the text you want to select.

The text you've selected will then be highlighted in gray.

If you need to select text that isn't touching you can do this by selecting your first section of text and then holding down the Ctrl key and selecting your second section of text using your mouse. (You can't arrow to the second section of text or you'll lose your already selected text.)

DROPDOWN MENU

If you right-click in a Word document, you will see what I'm going to refer to as a dropdown menu. (Sometimes it will actually drop upward if you're towards the bottom of the document.)

A dropdown menu provides you a list of choices to select from.

There are also dropdown menus available for some of the options listed under the tabs at the top of the screen. For example, if you go to the Home tab, you'll see small arrows below or next to some of the options, like the numbered list option in the paragraph section. If you click on those arrows, you'll see that there are multiple choices you can choose from listed on a dropdown menu.

DIALOGUE BOX

Dialogue boxes are pop-up boxes that cover specialized settings. As just mentioned, if you click on an expansion arrow, it will often open a dialogue box that contains more choices than are visible in that section. When you right-click in a Word document and choose Font, Paragraph, or Hyperlink that also opens dialogue boxes.

Dialogue boxes allow the most granular level of control over an option. For example, the Paragraph Dialogue Box has more options available than in the Paragraph section of the Home tab.

(This may not apply to you, but be aware that if you have more than one Word document open and open a dialogue box in one of those documents, you may not be able to move to the other documents you have open until you close the dialogue box.)

COLUMN

Excel uses columns and rows to display information. Columns run across the top of the worksheet and, unless you've done something funky with your settings, are identified using letters of the alphabet.

ROW

Rows run down the side of the worksheet and are numbered starting at 1 and up to a very high number.

CELL

A cell is a combination of a column and row that is identified by the letter of the column it's in and the number of the row it's in. For example, Cell A1 is the cell in the first column and first row of a worksheet.

SPREADSHEET

I'll try to avoid using this term, but if I do use it, I'll mean your entire Excel file. It's a little confusing because it can sometimes also be used to mean a specific worksheet, which is why I'll try to avoid it as much as possible.

WORKSHEET

This is the term I'll use as much as possible. A worksheet is a combination of rows and columns that you can enter data in. When you open an Excel file, it opens to worksheet one.

ABOUT THE AUTHOR

M.L. Humphrey is a former stockbroker with a degree in Economics from Stanford and an MBA from Wharton who has spent close to twenty years as a regulator and consultant in the financial services industry.

You can reach M.L. at mlhumphreywriter@gmail.com or at mlhumphrey.com.

www.ingramcontent.com/pod-product-compliance
Lightning Source LLC
LaVergne TN
LVHW080106070326
832902LV00014B/2458